Don't Do That!

By Janine Amos   Illustrated by Annabel Spenceley
Consultant Rachael Underwood

New Lenox
Public Library District
120 Veterans Parkway
New Lenox, Illinois 60451

Gareth Stevens Publishing
A WORLD ALMANAC EDUCATION GROUP COMPANY

Please visit our web site at: www.garethstevens.com
For a free color catalog describing Gareth Stevens Publishing's
list of high-quality books and multimedia programs, call
1-800-542-2595 (USA) or 1-800-387-3178 (Canada).
Gareth Stevens Publishing's fax: (414) 332-3567.

Library of Congress Cataloging-in-Publication Data

Amos, Janine.
    Don't do that! / by Janine Amos; illustrated by Annabel Spenceley.
       p. cm. — (Courteous kids)
    Includes bibliographical references.
    Summary: Two brief stories demonstrate the importance of telling someone
to quit when you do not like what they are doing, as well as telling them what
you would like for them to do instead.
    ISBN 0-8368-3605-7 (lib. bdg.)
    1. Social interaction in children—Juvenile literature.   2. Problem solving
in children—Juvenile literature.   [1. Behavior.   2. Etiquette.   3. Conduct of life.]
    I. Spenceley, Annabel, ill.   II. Title.
BF723.S62A465   2003
177'.1—dc21   2002036476

This edition first published in 2003 by
Gareth Stevens Publishing
A World Almanac Education Group Company
330 West Olive Street, Suite 100
Milwaukee, Wisconsin 53212 USA

3 1984 00204 7551

Series editor: Dorothy L. Gibbs
Graphic designer: Katherine A. Goedheer
Cover design: Joel Bucaro

This edition © 2003 by Gareth Stevens, Inc. First published by Cherrytree Press,
a subsidiary of Evans Brothers Limited. © 1999 by Cherrytree (a member of the
Evans Group of Publishers), 2A Portman Mansions, Chiltern Street, London
W1U 6NR, United Kingdom. This U.S. edition published under license from
Evans Brothers Limited. Additional end matter © 2003 by Gareth Stevens, Inc.

Printed in the United States of America

1 2 3 4 5 6 7 8 9 07 06 05 04 03

Note to Parents and Teachers

The questions that appear in **boldface** type can be used to initiate
discussion with your children or class. Encourage them to think of
possible answers before continuing with the story.

The New Rabbit

Josh has a new rabbit. He shows it to Levi.
"His name is Bouncer," says Josh.

"Can I hold him?" asks Levi.

Josh passes Bouncer to Levi.

Bouncer wriggles, so Levi squeezes him tightly.

"Don't do that!" shouts Josh. "You'll hurt him!"
How do you think Josh feels?

Josh tries to take Bouncer back.
"Let go, Levi!" he says.

The rabbit is frightened.

Levi lets go of Bouncer.
Josh holds the rabbit gently.

"I only wanted to hold him," says Levi.
How do you think Levi feels?

"Squeezing hurts rabbits," says Josh.
"You have to hold them like this."

Josh shows Levi how to hold Bouncer.
Levi pets the rabbit.

Then Levi holds Bouncer.
How do you think Levi feels now?

Red Toothpaste

Sasha is in the bathroom.
She sees the toothpaste. It's red!

18

Sasha squeezes the toothpaste.
She makes a design on the bathtub.

She makes a design on the wall.

She makes a design all along the hallway.

In Mommy's bedroom,
Sasha squeezes toothpaste on the mirror.

Leandra sees Sasha squeezing
the toothpaste. She also sees the mess.

23

"Don't do that!" shouts Leandra.

Sasha starts to cry.
How do you think Sasha feels?

25

Mommy rushes in.
"Look what Sasha has done!" says Leandra.

26

Mommy looks at the mess, then picks up Sasha.
How do you think Mommy feels?

27

"Sasha doesn't know about toothpaste yet," says
Mommy. "We need to show her what it's for."

Leandra gets her toothbrush.

"Look, Sasha," says Leandra.
"Toothpaste is for cleaning teeth."

Sasha grabs the toothbrush and grins.
She has no teeth to clean.

When people do things you don't like, letting them know is important. Saying "Don't do that!" is one way of telling people you don't like what they are doing. Telling them what you do want is even more helpful. Then they will know what you would like them to do.

More Books to Read

David Gets in Trouble. David Shannon (Blue Sky Press)

Rude Mule. Pamela Duncan Edwards (Henry Holt)

We Can Get Along: A Child's Book of Choices. Lauren Murphy Payne (Free Spirit)